Line Dance

Line Dance

Poems by Barbara Crooker

Word Press

Published by Word Press
P.O. Box 541106
Cincinnati, OH 45254-1106

ISBN: 9781933456928
LCCN: 2007940292

Poetry Editor: Kevin Walzer
Business Editor: Lori Jareo

Visit us on the web at www.word-press.com

Cover: Barbara Schaff, *Line of Nests (for Liese)*,
2004, Oil on panel, 13 X 59 inches, Private Collection.
www.barbaraschaff.com

Acknowledgments

America: "Euonymus alatus"
Atlanta Review: "Me 'n Bruce Springsteen Take My Baby off to College," "Hummingbird"
Artistry of Life: "Sunflowers"
Borderlands: "Simile," "Surface"
The Café Review: Americans in Paris: "Vol de Nuit," "When the Acacia Blooms,"
Chiron Review: "The Geography of Grief"
The Christian Century: "Euonymus alatus"
Christianity and Literature: "The VCCA Fellows Visit the Holiness Baptist Church, Amherst"
The Cresset: "One Song," "Rhythm Section"
Earth's Daughters: "Climbing the Jade Mountain"
The Healing Muse: "The Knot Garden"
The Journal of Poetry Therapy: "Blues for Karen"
Karamu: "Climbing the Eiffel Tower at Night," "Making Sense of the Sixties"
Literature and Belief: "Listen,"
The MacGuffin: "The Map of the World"
Margie/The American Journal of Poetry: "Les Faux Amis," "Poem on a Line by Anne Sexton"
New Works Review: "Valentine"
One Trick Pony: "Breath," "This Poem"
Passager: "Line Dance"
Pebble Lake Review: "45s, LPs"
Perspective: "Peony," "Ephemera"
Phoebe: "Things That Go Bump"
The Pittsburgh Post-Gazette: "The Slate Grey Junco"
Poetry East: "Gratitude"
Poetry International: "In the Camargue," "Gravy"
Poetry Motel: "Impermanent Joy"
Psychological Perspectives: "My Middle Daughter, on the Edge of Adolescence, Learns to Play the Saxophone"
Rattle: "Question Mark and the Mysterions"

RE:AL: "At the Poultry Reading"
RiverWind: "Miss Susan's Dance Academy"
Santa Fe Broadsides: "At the Thistle Feeder"
The Schuylkill Valley Review: "A Sonnet for Mr. Rutherford"
Sojourners: "Hard Bop"
Solo: "Eggplants"
Streetlight: "Leonid Meteor Shower"
The Texas Review: "Janis"
Triplopia: "*Les Effets de Neige*"
The Valparaiso Poetry Review: "Lemons"
West Branch: "Concerning Things That Can Be Doubled," "All Souls' Day"
Willow Review: "The Lowest Common Denominator"
Windhover: "Lemons"
The Writer: "Arabesque"
Zone 3: "Zero at the Bone"

"Concerning Things That Can Be Doubled" also appeared in the *West Branch* Twentieth Anniversary Retrospective (Bucknell University Press). "Me 'n Bruce Springsteen Take my Baby off to College" appeared in *Mothers and Daughters: A Poetry Celebration* (Random House) and in *Common Wealth: Contemporary Poets on Pennsylvania* (Penn State University Press). "Climbing the Jade Mountain" appeared in *Poems for the Mountains* (Salt Marsh Pottery Press). "Me 'n Bruce Springsteen Take My Baby off to College" and "When the Acacia Blooms," appeared in *To Have and to Hold* (Time Warner). "One Song" was made into a limited edition broadside (*The Making of Peace*). "The Knot Garden" appeared in *On The Outskirts* (Inglis House Press). "Eggplants" appeared in *Crazed by the Sun: Ecstatic Poems.*

"Me 'n Bruce Springsteen Take my Baby off to College," "Climbing the Eiffel Tower at Night," and "My Middle Daughter, on the Edge of Adolescence, Learns to Play the Saxophone" appeared in *Greatest Hits 1980-2000* (Pudding House Publications).

"Climbing the Eiffel Tower at Night" won the *Karamu* poetry contest. "Breath" was a Pushcart nominee. "Me 'n Bruce Springsteen Take My Baby off to College" won an International Merit Award from *The Atlanta Review*. "Line Dance" won honorable mention in the *Passager* poetry contest. "My Middle Daughter, on the Edge of Adolescence, Learns to Play the Saxophone" was read on *The Writer's Almanac* by Garrison Keillor.

Many thanks to the Pennsylvania Council on the Arts for grants, to the Virginia Center for the Creative Arts for the gift of space and silence, to my friends in writing, Barbara Reisner, Kathy Moser, Diane Lockward, and Geri Rosenzweig for their unwavering support, and to my children, Stacey, Rebecca, David, and my grandson, Daniel.

Table of Contents

Toujours, pour Richard

Dance, when you're broken open,
Dance, if you've torn the bandage off.
Dance in the middle of the fighting.
Dance in your blood.
Dance, when you're perfectly free.
~Rumi

Line Dance

At my daughter's wedding, we formed a chain
to *New York, New York,*
her friends from college arm in arm with my
ex-mother-in-law, who's whooping it up—

she loves Frank Sinatra—and she's holding
hands with the bride, whose elbow hooks
into a bridesmaid's—all four of them, in navy
shantung, have their arms around

each other's waists, a chorus kick line,
the groom's sister also holding
a bottle of beer; my youngest daughter
at the end, hair, a glory of red ringlets,

her arm's around the bride's half-sister,
who's giggling in embarrassment, and she's
connected to my childhood friend in a black
sheath, who holds onto the khaki sports coat

of my writing friend's husband, the dentist, while
his wife, in lilac, wraps her arm around one of
my neighbors, who's linked to a friend from
college in slinky silk slacks,

and there, at the end, is my ex-husband,
the one who didn't want to be married any
more, holding *his* soon-to-be-estranged second
wife, the one he left us for, at arm's length. *Start*

spreading the news: everyone I've ever loved
is here today, even the dead, raising a glass
and dancing, circling around the bride
in her frothy gown, bubbles rising
in a fluted glass, spilling out, running over.

I

Breath

The morning of my father's death, I was to leave
my family, travel south, work alone for a week.
How can you do this, he'd asked on previous trips,
You won't be home to fix dinner.
He thought I should cook stews and casseroles,
label and stack them in the freezer. This time,
the car was already packed with manuscripts,
books, and computer; it was as if even death
could not stop him from reaching out to hold me
back. *Stay home. How can you leave your family?*

The last time I saw him, it was early January,
white puffy clouds, pale blue sky, like his hair
and eyes. The temperature hovered near zero,
but the sky looked milky, benign. Near the end,
his breath was forced through a respirator,
stopping his speech. His eyes were mild
as a baby's, full of love the tongue could not
express. This was the best he could do.
Through the narrow window, the cold sky
stretched blameless, white and blue, behind him.

Blues for Karen

God does not leave us comfortless.
—Jane Kenyon

The season of your death, morning glories trailed
along the wire fence, one tone deeper than the sky.
I still go to the telephone to call you,
but the lines don't stretch to heaven—
the title of a bad country & western song.
How could you die? We weren't done talking yet.
So I am trying to call you using the morning glories,
whose blue mouths are open to the sky,
whose throats are white stars,
thinking those tendrils could trellis upward,
hand over little green hand, so tenacious,
they hang on in any storm,
forgetting that the quick slap of frost
will put out those blue lights,
that the seasons will snap shut like a purse,
that this old blue world will keep on spinning,
without you.

The Geography of Grief

Grief fills the room up
of my absent child.
—William Shakespeare

For you have entered another country,
gotten a visa, gone to live, where we,
your friends, have no passport, can only
be tourists. You send us notes on cards
postmarked Purgatory:
The map of this country defies cartography,
there are no expressways or shortcuts.
Instead, you must come to the City of Grief
as an immigrant, someone who has come to dwell,
be ready to stay a long time. The borders
are vague and indefinite, no checkpoints
or guard posts, difficult to tell
when you've entered or left. And the coasts,
too, are uncharted, rocky shoals, desolate reefs.
Throw away the guidebooks. Enter on your knees.
Go past the shores of mourning. See how loss
has shaped the topography, each contour line.
The map of the heart has no relief.

for Don and Jean

"The Map of the World, 1630," by Henricus Hondius

Here, the new world does not exist, lies somewhere
beyond the borders of vegetation, globed fruits:
grapes, melons, apples, the known demarcations.
Somewhere in Corsica, my ancestors
work the land, raise olives, picking them
by hand from twisted trees. Time's cartographer
has been at work on the parchment of their skin;
rivers and their tributaries run blue towards the sea
down the delta of their hands. He has etched
the province of their mouths and the forehead's
terrain with parallel lines, prime meridians.
Their world does not extend beyond day's end,
the glass of *grappa*, food put by for winter,
burlap sacks of chestnuts resting by the stove.
How could they imagine a passport, red and gold,
the towering stone forests of the *terra nova*
that would one day fill the horizon past the railing
of the *SS Nord America*, where a small eleven-year-
old girl, my grandmother, recorded only as part
of the baggage of her brother, Gaetano,
finally reaches the shore.

The Knot Garden

For David

In my son's brain, sounds travel on a difficult
journey through cortex and cerebellum, arrive
with distortions, different clusters of word
associations, as if they were travelers hacking
their way through a hedge or a thicket
in unknown territory. We're never certain
that what we say arrives at the station on time,
the train screeching its brakes, discharging
passengers. Autism's a labyrinth of false twists
and turns, blind passageways, spirals that lead
nowhere. Here, chevrons of geese wedge
their way across the sky each autumn; they know
where they are going, have purchased tickets
marked "South." Our route is more circuitous:
two steps forward, one step back, a knot garden
where the possibilities diminish as the years
branch on. Too soon, we'll arrive at the alpine
altitudes where the vegetation's scarce, the flowers
tiny but exquisite, the foliage barely visible.

Les Effets de Neige: Impressionists in Winter

Exhibit at The Phillips Collection, Washington, DC

When they tired of painting sun and wind,
they turned to fog, ice, and snow, tried to find
some other way to catch the light, to pin it down,
a brooch on a dress or a nail in a barn.
How many different tubes of paint
are there for white?

Camille Monet glances at us over her shoulder,
framed by the gauzy curtains, shrouded in snow.
Caillebotte's chimneys exhale, like glamorous
women in a café. Pissarro piled snow
on his rooftops, slabs of cake thick with fondant.
Sisley fell in love with shadows, all those cool
blue notes, while Gauguin forsook the hot light
of Tahiti for thatched huts in Brittany, snow
slipping from the eaves.

Soon, another cold front will move in
from the west, turning the air crystalline,
and they will go at it again: a flurry of brush
strokes, a snow squall of new paintings
shivering on their easels.

The Slate Grey Junco

with his immaculate bib, sooty jacket,
bobs in the snow for sunflower seeds.
Caught between two needs, hunger and shelter,
he keeps coming back, even as the arctic wind
shuttles him like the cock in a badminton game,
wind that rattles the windows, shakes the house,
and blows the snow in great sheets across the yard.
But here he is again, charcoal wings beating hard,
as he skids off the barbecue lid, comes in
for another landing. What comes back? Memory
and desire, my grandmother, long gone, the empty
rooms in my parents' house, voices of friends
beyond the reach of wires,
white thread in a bobbin, a chain of stitching,
the line of waves along the shore.
Fugue and variations, the wind's refrain.
Snow, folding back
on itself, warping and woofing
the scarf of the storm.

Zero at the Bone

The scouring light of winter
scrubs whatever it falls on,
the bright whiteness revealing
all the small incursions,
marks and stains of another year.
In the bare bones of trees, we see
old nests, broken branches, bagworm,
gall, all that was hidden by summer's
green scrim. Now we are at the heart
of things, the bone chill
of zero, the closed eye
of the pond. No secrets.
Only stories the wind brings
as it howls down chimneys,
whistles through eaves.
This is the blank text of the snow,
these are the unwritten lines.
The journey without a ticket,
the century running out of time,
the heart's arithmetic: nada nada nada.

Valentine

The heart is devious above all else; it is perverse—
who can understand it?
—Jeremiah 17:9

It's the beginning of February, winter's ash end.
No flowers blooming. I've hung hearts
in all the windows: red glass, stamped clay,
beveled prism, woven willow strips.
Thirty years ago, my first-born came and went
in one brief day. Now, the snow is busy, composing
its small white music, the little notes tumbling
off the staff. The heart wants and wants and wants
some more. Spring so far in the distance,
it will never arrive. Those babies in the nursery,
pink and blue blossoms. Grief and heart could be
the same word; both have five letters, both rhyme
with blood. Snow is the mute language of loss.

Lemons

A yellow sun splashed lavish light
on the garden, a bright bloom
of a morning, full of possibility.
I was away from home, teaching,
when one of the poems peeled
away the thin rind of memory,
and there I was, back
in the maternity ward
when my first-born died.

I remember how white and cold
the room was, even though
my friends brought flowers:

irises, roses. I was hollow,
a fruit that had been pulped
for juice, leaving nothing
but a shell, no flesh, no seeds.

Thirty years later, my daughter's
globed stomach, and then, there
was Daniel, shining and puckered
in the moony glow of the delivery
room, rinsed with light from another
world, and a new day dawning.

II

Line

not what someone hands you in a bar
along with the shaker of salt and a lime.
And not what you use to go fishing,
that flexible invisible filament
that bisects the air between water and sky.
I'm not talking about queuing up,
or the little etchings time's fingernails
have scratched on my face. Nor do I mean
the rope you hang clothes on, those wooden
pegs all in a row, or what you toe or risk or hit
with a bat, straight as the train tracks out of town.
No, I'm saying this: the spine, the matrix, the core
of what's laid down, then played over and over,
improvised, embroidered, embellished.
I love the way it moves away and then comes back,
finds itself again, the hard line, the official line,
the line of scrimmage, one down, goal to go.

Poem on a Line by Anne Sexton, "We are All Writing God's Poem"

Today, the sky's the soft blue of a work shirt washed
a thousand times. The journey of a thousand miles
begins with a single step. On the interstate listening
to NPR, I heard a Hubble scientist
say, "The universe is not only stranger than we
think, it's stranger than we *can* think." I think
I've driven into spring, as the woods revive
with a loud shout, redbud trees, their gaudy
scarves flung over bark's bare limbs. Barely doing
sixty, I pass a tractor trailer called *Glory Bound*,
and aren't we just? Just yesterday,
I read Li Po: "There is no end of things
in the heart," but it seems like things
are always ending—vacation or childhood,
relationships, stores going out of business,
like the one that sold jeans that really fit—
And where do we fit in? How can we get up
in the morning, knowing what we do? But we do,
put one foot after the other, open the window,
make coffee, watch the steam curl up
and disappear. At night, the scent of phlox curls
in the open window, while the sky turns red violet,
lavender, thistle, a box of spilled crayons.
The moon spills its milk on the black tabletop
for the thousandth time.

Surface

If you want to know all about Andy Warhol,
just look at my films and paintings and me.
There's nothing behind it. That's all there is.
—Andy Warhol

It *is* all surface, isn't it, the thin blue silk of the sky,
an oak leaf's chlorophyll production line,
the unblinking eye of the pond? When I was
as shallow as an undergraduate could possibly be,
I peeled off from a field trip to Soho galleries
to visit The Factory; my friend and I nearly
identical in our veneers: ironed hair, wheat jeans,
black sleeveless shells, our unwavering scorn
of the outside world . . . .

It was dazzling, every surface painted silver:
the walls, ceilings, tables, chairs, bathroom
fixtures, like walking into a roll of aluminum foil.
And Andy—thin, spectral, white blond hair,
black sunglasses, nearly wordless. Mostly, he just
was, the Zen of non-being, the art of perfect
detachment. And we were mute, too, inarticulate
in our youth. We knew what it was we *didn't* want,
but not what we did.

Now, all these years and lives later, the twisting
and turning of many roads—some macadam,
some asphalt, some stone—I can't remember
her name, just how straight her hair was,
how it hung down her back like a bolt of cloth.
In the untidy closet of my heart, I think about
what we put on, fashion, facade, how many layers
we need between our skin and the rest of the world.

Simile

My son showed me his paper from remedial
English; he was supposed to fill in the blanks:
Cool as a _________.
Smooth as a ________. Neat as a _____.

He came up with: angry as a teakettle,
and when I asked, “Why? ” said,
“Because it was boiling mad.” Of course,
it was marked wrong, one more red mark
in his life’s long test.

When I called from Virginia to ask him
what he did last weekend,
he said, “We bought Italian salad dressing.”

Last fall we went to a Broadway
play; what he liked the most
were traffic lights and *Don’t Walk* signs.

Oh, my little pork chop, my sweet potato,
my tender tot. You have made me pay attention
to the world’s smallest minutia. My pea-shaped
heart, red as a stop sign, swells, fills with
the helium of tenderness, thinks it might burst.

Concerning Things That Can Be Doubled

Dutch jump rope, two girls in braids
twirling the ropes until they blur.
Crosses, dares, talk, or its fancy French
cousin, *entendre*. Header, date, breasted
serge suit. Team, time, troubles. It's this,
or nothing. Boiler, barrel, bed, the blind's
bind that puts us in jeopardy. Cattle brands.
Shots of Scotch. Decker buses. You.
And here I am, of two minds on the subject,
slowly rocking and talking to myself.

Les Faux Amis

another name for false cognates,
French words that resemble English ones
but have very different meanings

Not the ones that are easy to confuse, like *journée*
(day) and journey *(voyage)*
or *cave* (wine cellar) and cave *(caverne)*
or the ones that are harder,

brassière (baby's vest) and brassiere *(soutien-*
gorge), *magasin* (department store)
and magazine *(magazine),* but the friends you
thought were yours, just a phone call

or e-mail away, but weren't. Or the double-*crème*
fromage that now raises
your cholesterol, or the *vin rouge* that puts
your head in a vise the next day.

How many betrayals *(les trahisons)* do we have to
endure? There's the *editeur*
who receives your best work, only to send it back
with "sorry"

scrawled on every page. Does it sound better
in French, "*Je suis désolé?*"
Which is not to say desolate, inconsolable
(inconsolable). There are consolations

in this life, children, cats, *chocolat.* You can rip
those slips into a thousand pieces,
la neige, let them pile into drifts in the compost
with the broken eggs and orange peels.

And while there are friends who whisper
down the alley, who don't return your calls,
holiday cards, who drift off, *cendres*
from a campfire, *fumée* in the wind,

there are more who remain: *les roches dures, vrais*
bleu, loyal, fidèle.

Vol de Nuit / Night Flight

Now, isn't that more elegant than
taking the Red-Eye?
And don't you love it when the flight attendant
(Remember when she used to be a stewardess?
When everything matched her uniform,
even her luggage, and her makeup was heavy
and impeccable?) hands out pillows, blankets
soft as babies' dreams, eye masks,
ear plugs—everything Mother would do
but tuck you in and read you a story.
Or maybe she does—think of the fable
she recites at the beginning of the flight.
Or did you think it was true, that oxygen
miraculously drops from above if the cabin
pressure fails? That your seat cushion becomes
a life preserver if you fall into the black night
of the North Atlantic? That emergency lights
will twinkle and glow, illuminate your path
to the exit chute, little constellations of hope?
Never mind. Relax into your backrest
of many positions. Enjoy the multi-course
many-sectioned meal brought to you hot,
without a kitchen in sight. Hear the tinkle
of the cart as she progresses down the aisle,
those cunning little bottles. Put on your headset,
find the channel with jazz or blues, unscrew
the metal top, sip your red, and *voilà*,
you're in Paris already, hours ahead of time.
So the *pâté* and *camembert* come in tin foil,
and the roll's hard as an iceberg. Thousands
of miles are rushing under your feet
beneath these silver wings. Soon,
you'll be racing the dawn, as morning throws
her rosy covers over the sky. *Briôches,*
câfé au lait, croissants and *café noir* will roll
down the aisles. You'll begin your long descent
from the land of the clouds. Things
may have shifted overhead. Everyone is speaking

in tongues, and none of them are yours.
You must go to *le contrôle de passeports,*
and you will need to declare: business
or pleasure. Someone is meeting you
at the gate; he's carrying a baguette
and a single red rose, knows the minute
your plane touches the tarmac.
Now you have reclaimed your luggage,
passed through customs, and entered
the terminal, where the rest
of your life is waiting.

Climbing the Eiffel Tower at Night,

flood-lit, so the traceries of girder and beam
seem insubstantial, a conjurer's vision,
an airy web spun out of light. It's a pyramid of X's,
row on row of kisses curving up to the sky,
meeting at the vanishing point, where all things
come together.

Premier étage:
We climb into this ladder of light.
Below, the sycamore trees have stripped
down to bar and girder, a complicated
fretwork of branches, dropped their leaves
in a heap of gold on the ground.
The sinuous loops of the Seine
wind around their feet,
wrap the city in a silver ribbon.

Deuxième étage:
Dizzy with height, for a moment things
reverse, and it's the night sky spread
below us, darkness pooled at our feet,
pierced with different constellations,
a new mythology.

Troisième étage:
This high up, the air is cold, clouds go racing by.
One minute the lights wink out, the next,
they're back again, the clouds whipping
around our heads like a dancer's gauzy veil.
We kiss, wrapped in scarves of mist,
the lights go out again.

At the top of this thin edifice, a single needle,
like the sweet momentary joining of flesh.

Climbing the Jade Mountain

(filling out my son's SSI forms)

The Chinese poets tell us
that to start an impossible journey,
you must begin with small steps,
one foot in front of the other
on the rock-hard road. There are
no maps. The mountain gleams
in the afternoon sun. The load
grows increasingly heavy. We
are tired, we are thirsty,
and we want to know
how many dusty miles remain?
The mountain is silent.
All the guidebooks are written
in an ancient language
we don't understand.
When night overtakes us,
we lie down in a dry
river bed, with a stone
for a pillow. Morning
draws her curtains.
We start again.

This Poem

is a clothesline hanging
between two trees;
the words, hung by wooden
pegs, move with the wind.
Between the lines, punctuations
of iris, peonies, bleeding hearts,
and a meadow that stretches
as far as the pines. It has been raining
all night. Someone I once loved
appears in the margins; I no longer
remember his name. The wind roams
through the trees, and two crows
resume their argument, not caring
anymore who's wrong, who's right,
make inky tracks across the page.
The fog of memory blurs the text,
words running wild in the field.
I hear horns blowing, as the boat
comes into the harbor, my grandmother,
a small girl, looking over the rail
as the new world rises before her.
I smell steam rising from ironed cotton
as my mother slicks down the sheets.
The blank pages flap in the breeze,
their own kind of crazy dance.

III

Miss Susan's Dance Academy

I am seven, short for my age, round
as rotini, awkward and clumsy. My parents
think dance lessons might transform
their ugly duckling into, if not a swan,
perhaps a long-legged American rose.
Shuffle. Shuffle. Quickstep.
I scuff my shiny patent shoes every time
I brush my feet. My little taps sound nothing
like the raucous clatter of the June Taylor Dancers
on the Jackie Gleason Show.
Brush, brush, hop. Brush, brush, hop.

My clunky little body stayed pretty much
the same. Spring blew in—recital time.
Our mothers had to sew costumes from a picture,
were given bolts of cloth, no pattern. My class
followed our set pattern to tap tap tap
in two straight lines across the shellacked pine
floor. In the middle of the show, my side tippity-
tapped left, but I got confused, bolted right
off the stage, never to return. And so it started,
those elevators in the stomach, drum rolls
in the heart, the confirmation of the whispers,
the ones that say, *Your timing's off, you don't
measure up, you dance to a different drum.*

A Sonnet for Mr. Rutherford

In sixth grade, our mothers signed
us up for Mr. Rutherford's School of Dance
where we could learn ballroom dancing and
manners on the dull tile of the combined

cafeteria/auditorium each Thursday night.
We lined up: reluctant boys to the left,
girls in giggling knots to the right;
the fate we knew as worse than death

was odd one out, who partnered Mrs. R.,
stout and girdled, but she could waltz
and fox trot like Adele Astaire.
We learned to *look out for the dip,*

which, on life's circuitous travels,
was good advice. *Slow, slow, quick step.*

45s, LPs

My autistic son listens to the oldies,
digs that old time rock 'n roll rhythm & blues.
My husband says it's like our teen years
are hanging out in his room, coming
from the radio—*When the night is dark,*
and the land is far and the moon
is the only light you see—
rolling up the sleeves of their black tee shirts,
collapsing on the bed in a froth of petticoats,
what's left on the beach when a wave
subsides and the tide begins to ebb,
plants a kiss on the shore, then rolls
out to sea, and the sea is very still once more.
Baby oil and iodine shine on our arms
and legs, lemon juice in our hair,
plastic transistor radios tuned to The Top Ten.
Get outta that kitchen and rattle them pots 'n pans.
What misfired neurons cause him to shake
and fidget his fingers before his eyes,
call out in class when the teacher's talking,
be out of synch with everyone else?
Up on the roof it's peaceful
as can be, and there the world below
can't bother me. When we're gone, what then?
What slot will he fit into like a quarter
slipping in a jukebox for three plays,
slow songs you could dance to all night long?

How Many Trees Have Died for This Poem?

Someone on my poetry list says publishing a poem
is like dropping rose petals in the Grand Canyon.
How different, then, I ask, is writing one?
My autistic son plays a game where he writes
the alphabet in the sand, letter by letter, then lets
the waves' eraser wipe it clean, starts over. It's all
sea wrack and fish foam, tide strew and shell
scrawl anyway— Does the world want another
poem? Maybe the best place to write is the blue slate
of the sky, where the words can linger until a front
comes by with its squall line of clouds. Maybe
the ideal audience is grass and leaves, all that green
knowledge. The moon shuts off its flashlight
under the covers of night,
and we all go to bed in the dark.

The VCCA Fellows Visit the Holiness Baptist Church, Amherst, Virginia

We are the only light faces in a sea of mahogany,
tobacco, almond, and this is not the only way
we are different. We've come in late, the choir
already singing, swaying to the music, moving
in the spirit. *When I was down, Lord, when*
I was down, Jesus lifted me. And, for a few minutes,
we are raised up, out of our own skepticism
and doubts, rising on the swell of their voices.
The singers sit, and we pass the peace, wrapped
in thick arms, ample bosoms, and I start to think
maybe God is a woman of color, and that She loves
us, in spite of our pale selves, so far away
from who we should really be. Parishioners
give testimonials, a deacon speaks of his sister,
who's "gone home," and I realize he doesn't mean
back to Georgia, but that she's passed over. I float
on this sweet certainty, of a return not to the bland
confection of wispy clouds and angels in nightshirts,
but to childhood's kitchen, a dew-drenched June
morning, roses tumbling by the back porch.
The preacher mounts the lectern, tells us he's been
up since four working at his other job, the one
that pays the bills, and he delivers a sermon
that lightens the heart, unencumbered by dogma
and theology. For the benediction, we all join hands,
visitors and strangers enfolded in the whole,
like raisins in sweet batter. We step through the door
into the stunning sunshine, and our hearts
lift out of our chests, tiny birds flying off to light
in the redbuds, to sing and sing and sing.

Listen,

I want to tell you something. This morning
is bright after all the steady rain, and every iris,
peony, rose, opens its mouth, rejoicing.
I want to say, wake up, open your eyes, there's
a snow-covered road ahead, a field of blankness,
a sheet of paper, an empty screen. Even
the smallest insects are singing, vibrating
their entire bodies, tiny violins of longing
and desire. We were made for song.
I can't tell you what prayer is, but I can take
the breath of the meadow into my mouth,
and I can release it for the leaves' green need.
I want to tell you your life is a blue coal, a slice
of orange in the mouth, cut hay in the nostrils.
The cardinals' red song dances in your blood.
Look, every month the moon blossoms
into a peony, then shrinks to a sliver of garlic.
And then it blooms again.

Peony

Imagine the hard knot of its bud,
all that pink possibility.
Day by day it visibly swells,
doubles, until one morning in June,
it unfolds, ruffle after ruffle, an explosion
of silk. Imagine your breath, as it runs
through your body, how it ebbs and flows,
a river of air. Imagine the exotic bazaar
of the kitchen, where fragrances—star anise,
cloves, cardamom—jostle, fill your nostrils
with the colors of the orient. Imagine
a feather, how it caresses your spine, the shoulder
blades, the place where wings might have been.
Imagine your heart, how it works like a clock,
midnight to noon, never punches in,
never takes a vacation, keeps tolling, keeps toiling,
like black ants on this peony, whose true job
is to gather all the sweetness they can muster,
to do their small part to carry
the breath of the world.

In the Camargue,

there are flamingos everywhere—*les roses*
flamants, literally, pink flames—wading
in the shallows, dabbling in the reeds.
Their supercilious beaks, Roman noses,
give them an air of disdain
as they stalk the marshes, straining
small mollusks through their soup
spoon bills, half pink, half black,
the colors of a 60s Cadillac.
Their loopy necks curve in question marks,
their skinny stilty legs, hot pink exclamations
under the wide black vee of their opened wings.
You'd think Rube Goldberg designed these birds—
their improbable gawky take-off, running on water,
jerky as puppets—this will never fly—but then,
they do, these pink blossoms, these sunsets
on the wing, these rose flames in the sky.

Arabesque

She sat at a small café in Paris, sunlight
filtering through the plane trees,
a dance of shadow and leaf.
Café filtré shimmered
in its small white cup.
At the Jardin de Luxembourg,
there were roses everywhere,
crinkled and ruched flirts
that sent their perfume
in envelopes of scent
on the soft air.
She was writing a letter,
but the words wouldn't come;
there was so much blue distance
between them. Up in the trees,
turtledoves blew their low notes,
songs flew easily from their beaks.
O, this dance of love, how it twists
and curlicues, the art deco sign
above the Métro, the many pathways
that wind to the heart.

Impermanent Joy

. . . calling up that constant possibility: impermanent joy.
—Diane Leffler

The Egyptian word for love is "long desire,"
and I am full of such a long desire for you
and all that is lovely between woman and man.
I want to wear your scent on me as easily
as night puts on her black silk slip.

Some nights, I wish I were single,
the way you eat apples in bed,
the fights, words that can't be
taken back that fly from our mouths
like a flock of crows.

A man and a woman speaking different dialects,
Mandarin and Cantonese, and only the calligraphy
of words is the same, so far apart are nuance
and meaning, shadows and shade.
Sometimes we speak the language of the body,
dancing in the dark; how close we come together,
how far we are apart.

IV

One Song

after Rumi

A cardinal, the very essence of red, stabs
the hedgerow with his piercing notes;
a chickadee adds three short beats,
part of the percussion section,
and a white-throated sparrow
moves the melody along.
Last night, at a concert, crashing waves
of Prokofiev; later, soft rain falling
steadily and a train whistle off in the distance.
And today, the sun, waiting for its cue,
comes out from the clouds for a short sweet
solo, then sits back down, rests between turns.
On the other side of the world, night's black
bass fiddle rosins its bow, draws it
over the strings, resonates with the breath
of sleepers, animal, vegetable, human.
All the world breathes in, breathes out.
It hums, it throbs, it improvises.
So many voices. Only one song.

At the Thistle Feeder, Finches, Little Chips of Sun,

hang upside down, then flit from branch
to branch in the cherry tree,
which has been whipped
to a froth, blossoms
on even the smallest twig,
a whole rococo palace
of a tree. Lazy drowse of bees.
The air so sugary,
it makes your teeth ache.
A downy woodpecker goes up and down
the trunk, tick-tick, tick-tick. Light hangs
in the balance, like the truce in the east,
fragile, temporary. The sky wavers
over our heads, a flag of blue silk;
grass unrolls its green rug at our feet.
Peace, elusive as bird song,
flutters away.

Gratitude

This week, the news of the world is bleak,
another war grinding on, and all these friends
down with cancer, or worse, a little something
long term that they won't die of for twenty
or thirty miserable years— And here I live
in a house of weathered brick, where a man
with silver hair still thinks I'm beautiful.
How many times have I forgotten
to give thanks? The late day sun
shines through the pink wisteria with its green
and white leaves as if it were stained glass,
there's an old cherry tree that one lucky Sunday
bloomed with a rainbow: cardinals, orioles,
goldfinches, blue jays, indigo buntings,
and my garden has tiny lettuces just coming up,
so perfect they could make you cry: Green Towers,
Red Sails, Oak Leaf. For this is May, and the whole
world sings, gleams, as if it were basted in butter,
and the air's sweet enough to send a diabetic into
shock— And at least today, all the parts of my body
are working, the sky's clear as a china bowl, leaves
murmur their leafy chatter, finches percolate
along. I'm doodling around this page, know
sorrow's somewhere beyond the horizon, but still
I'm riffing on the warm air, the wing beats of my lungs
that can take this all in, flush the heart's red peony,
then send it back without effort or thought.
And the trees breathe in what we exhale,
clap their green hands in gratitude, bend to the sky.

When the Acacia Blooms,

bees go crazy, get drunk on the honey-soaked air.
I think I could sit here forever, inhaling

this sweetness, thinking about the time we sat
in sunlight filtered by its twice-compound

leaves, some small village in France,
the name now faded ink on the back

of a snapshot. What I remember is the sun,
how it licked our arms and faces like a rough-

tongued cat, how everything was aureate
that spring afternoon, like walking into a painting;

how we shared a sandwich, *jambon et fromage,*
your hand covered mine, and I thought

of the night before, our small room, how we
climbed the ladder of each other's body

until the stars showered us with sparks,
and then we fell . . . .Where today, this scent

of wisteria, purple racemes falling from twisted
vines, reminds me of acacia in the warm April sun,

so thick you could spread it on toast or bottle it
in glass jars. Off in the distance, doves call,

their long vowels not mournful, but one of those
sounds that taps into memory's underground river,

this waterfall of flowers, pouring its hot breath
onto the stunned air.

Hummingbird

He comes every day in his crushed-emerald cape,
flashing in front of the kitchen window, quick
as a thought and just as elusive; one blink,
and he's gone. Try to show him to your mother
who's come by for tea; she doesn't turn quickly
enough, doesn't see his throat, red as a stoplight,
doesn't see him dart in and out of the bee balm,
honeysuckle, trumpet vine. Her skin is thin
as a folded road map; she's setting off on a new
journey. The tea trembles in its porcelain boat.
She is getting ready to board a great white ship
whose sails are already luffing in the wind;
the hawsers creak and groan, the crew
is ready to cast off. But she is still casting on,
yarn the color of spring grass, yarn the color
of heart's blood, knitting afghan squares
for the homeless. She sips her tea. He flickers
back into view, takes a long sweet drink.
He signals *stop*, then *go*; *stop*, then *go*,
both directions at once, confusing semaphores
that spark and crackle in the brilliant, merciless sun.

Sunflowers

The sunflower
cannot change what it is, it will always
turn toward the sun.
—Tu Fu, "Feng-Hsien Return Chant"

In French, they are *les tournesols*, and they do,
they do, they turn to the sun, follow the white-hot
disc on its daily rounds. At night, no light, they nod
their sleepy heads, let their shoulders slump,
then face the east with hope each dawn. Brown-
eyed, yellow-rayed, they rasp in the wind,
a whole section of cellos. Once, driving
around a bend, I came across a field of them
bobbing, the blue sky waving madly behind.
I wanted to stay, learn their language of oily seeds
and scratchy stalks, let the wind move through
my green arms, lift my yellow hair, toss it this way
and that, my feet firm in the dirt. *Feel the earth,*
the yoga teacher exhorts on my tape. *Feel the pulse*
of the planet. Be the pulse. I nod, heavy-headed,
and heft my burden of light.

Eggplants

We start as purple stars in a deep green firmament,
swell into fullness as the summer sun fills
July afternoons, then blooms white hot,
washing the blue right out of the sky.

Cradle us in the palm of your hand,
solid and fleshy, glossy as satin,
as we pull our black camisoles
over ample curves, rounded hips.

We spring from the dirt in greenness,
we return in dust or compost, but oh! what
a lovely dance there is in between, bobbing
on spiky stems in the hot wind,
our wine-dark skin hot to the touch.
Come, sway with us, in the dark.

Ephemera

For whoever has despised the day of small things?
—Zechariah 4:10

It's just a day when dusty sycamore leaves
flash silver as they scull in the wind,
when high clouds journey across the sky,
huge white blossoms going to seed.
It's summer, and the world exhales its green breath.
For once, the humidity machine's been shut off,
and the air feels like a lover's caress.
My grouchy white cat stalks through the high grass,
twines once around my legs, then sits nearby,
as close as he's ever going to get. A spider
casts her filaments on a frond of Russian sage,
finches go to work on the sunflower heads.
In the meadow, the traffic of ants and bees . . . .

The sun, no longer last week's hot griddle,
casts us in a bronzy light, turns the air to syrup.
I neither want to be here, nor there. The afternoon
grows luminous around the edges. Dinner
on the porch: a thick steak, matchstick asparagus,
many-grained bread. A wedge of chocolate cake
cut in two, a handful of raspberries.
And, in the twilight, swallows scissor
the air over the orchard, cutting scraps
in the cloth of light, and we sip
the last few mouthfuls of wine, the small
pleasures of the night, the amplitude of the day.

The Lowest Common Denominator

My son and I sit at the kitchen table,
working with fractions. He doesn't see
the need to reduce, would just as soon let
12/16 or 8/24 live in their binomial splendor
rather than pare them down
to austere quarters or thirds.

I am thinking about literature,
how it all can be reduced
to love or loss
when you get right down
to the heart.

Let's let X mark the spot.
See Spot run. Oh, Jane,
where is Puff? Where is Baby Sally?
I am Jane, in a plaid cotton dress
with a Peter Pan collar, sturdy shoes.
Now I have a child with,
as they say, global delays,
which means a kindergartner playing
in the body of a spotty adolescent.

What equation can we use
to find his place in the world? $d = C/\pi$?

Oh, he's happy as pie when he sits
on the driveway with a map of, say,
New Jersey, plotting imaginary trips.
Take I-78 east to route 611 south . . . .

And off we go, on our careening journey.
When death, that great subtracter, comes,
what will happen then? Only love,
the common denominator of the kitchen
table, will remain.

Euonymus alatus

Outside my window, the bushes have turned, redder
than any fire, and the sky is the same blue Giotto
used for Mary's robes. My mother says if she still
had a house, she'd plant one or two of these bushes,
and I love how she's still thinking about gardening,
as if she were in the middle of the story,
even though we both know she's at the end.
Down in the meadow, the goldenrod's gone
from cadmium yellow to a feathery beige,
the ghost of itself. Mother, too, fades away,
skin thin as the tissue stuffed
up her sleeve. The scars on her stomach
itch and burn, but inside, she's still the girl
who loved to turn cartwheels, the woman
whose best days were on fairways and putting
greens. On television, we watch California
go up in smoke, flames leapfrogging ridge to ridge.
Here, these leaves release a shower of scarlet
feathers, as everything starts to let go. Oh, how this
world burns and burns us, yet we are not consumed.

Things That Go Bump

I terrified my little brother
by telling him that crocodiles
swam in the swampy carpet between
our beds; their huge reptilian jaws,
glittering teeth, immense hunger
for tiny toes kept him in his bed, all night.
Howdy Doody and Buffalo Bob, their disembodied
heads bobbing along the ceiling, our little gods,
looked down on us from the wallpaper border,
frowned at my bold-faced lies.

Later, there would be the Tunnel of Love,
which wasn't, but rather, a dank passage smelling
of cellar, where sudden turns and bursts of light—
with dangling hairy spiders or pointing skeletons—
might make you throw yourself at the boy you rode
in with, let him put his bony arms around your neck.
We needed Bruce Springsteen to sing us the dark:
The house is haunted and the ride gets rough,
You've got to learn to live with what you can't rise above.

And then we rose up into the real world,
where passenger planes could be used as missiles,
where the tallest buildings could collapse in a pile
of rubble and dust. . . .where The Troubles, be they
in Ireland or the Middle East, never end, peaces
and truces crumbling like castles of shells and sand.

My mother said, "*It's only the dark; when you grow*
up, you'll see, there's nothing to be afraid of,"
but now I have, and I don't.

Me ’n Bruce Springsteen Take My Baby off to College

for Stacey

We hit the turnpike early, O Thunder Road,
every inch of the car packed: sweatshirts, prom
gowns, teddy bears, such heavy baggage.
She’s both coming and going, this shy violet
of a child, the teenager too hostile
to be in the same room, breathe the same air.
Now she dozes beside me as the car spools up
the miles, and I slip in a favorite tape, raise
the volume. Her skin, edible, a downy peach,
her long hair unwinding. My foot taps
the accelerator with the beat; the Big Man,
Clarence Clemons, pours his soul out his sax,
yearning, throbbing, as the turnpike pulls us west,
bisecting Pennsylvania, tunneling through
the mountains: Blue, Allegheny, Kittatinny,
Tuscarora, this big-muscled, broad-backed
hunk of a state.

We drive deeper into the heart of anthracite,
the wind blows through the dark night of her hair.
A harmonica wails and whines, brings me
back to my tie-dyed college years; sex looms
like a Ferris wheel, carnival lights in the water,
but we've reached our exit, here she is,
it’s independence day, ready or not, Pittsburgh,
city of smoke and grit, polished chrome
and glass, soot streaked buildings, pocket

handkerchief neighborhoods, abandoned
steelworks, the Monongahela River.
I deliver her again, heavier this time.
We set up the room, she turns cocky and sulky,
breaks into sobs when I leave.

On the return trip, I play the same tapes over
and over. The miles roll by, I'm driven by the beat,
everybody's got a hungry heart, nearly there:
Lenhartsville, Krumsville, Kutztown,
green rolling hills dotted with cows,
Pittsburgh's iron and steel filling the horizon
in the rear view mirror.

My Middle Daughter, on the Edge of Adolescence, Learns to Play the Saxophone

for Rebecca

Her hair, that halo of red gold curls,
has thickened, coarsened,
lost its baby fineness,
and the sweet smell of childhood
that clung to her clothes
has just about vanished.
Now she's getting moody,
moaning about her hair,
clothes that aren't the right brands,
boys that tease.
She clicks over the saxophone keys
with gritty fingernails polished
in pink pearl, grass stains
on the knees of her sister's old
designer jeans. She's gone
from sounding like the smoke detector
through Old MacDonald and Jingle Bells.
Soon she'll master these keys,
turn notes into liquid gold,
wail that reedy brass.
Soon, she'll be a woman.
She's gonna learn to play the blues.

Making Sense of the Sixties

title of a PBS documentary

Maybe we weren't meant to.
Maybe those years weren't linear,
but a mandala or a kaleidoscope:
The Haight. Hearts and peace signs
painted on faces, on Volkswagens,
on used school buses. Blowing soap bubbles,
sailing Frisbees, dropping acid, smoking grass.
Day-glow. Viet Nam. The stutter of choppers.
Incoming. Burning villages. A polished black wall.
Selma. Montgomery. Kent State. The Kennedys,
gone; Martin and Malcolm, gone.
All the funeral trains. The mystery train.
The Magical Mystery Tour.
Children named Sunshine or Free.
When granola was exotic,
like sprouts or tofu or whole grain bread.
A brown fist, clenched, raised high.
A shining sea of waving arms.
Love beads, madras dresses, no bras.
Janis and Jimi and Cass.
When hair was a flag, long and straight
and ironed, or afro'd to a halo,
you knew who belonged,
who loved good music, who hated
the government. Plant daisies in all the rifles.
Wear the flag. Dance the dirty boogie.
Walk for peace, love, brotherhood.
Save the planet. Save the whales.
Keep marching.

Janis

She sang to all of us who never fit
in, too bony, too fat, too weird, wired
all wrong for the cliques of a Texas high
school, the religion of football, cheerleaders,
jocks; longnecks, pickup trucks, Madras
A-lines, bubble cuts, penny loafers.
What's amazing is she stayed as long as she did—
Take another little piece of my heart, now, baby—
When she sang, she put the pedal to the floor,
hundred miles an hour and a brick wall straight
ahead. And there was *nothing*
straight about this girl, hot pink feathers
flying out of her hair, silver bracelets
up to her elbows, chunky rings on every finger,
their own kind of ball and chain. Granny glasses,
glassy-eyed full-stoned grin. Voice like a rasp,
a jar full of nails, shaking.

If, in the end, it all went wrong, well, Janis,
you never just showed up, you always gave it
everything you had. *Look down on us*, now,
the acne-scarred, the greasy-haired, the unbeautiful.
Stomp your leg like a piston building up steam,
thrust and jut your skinny hips, shimmy and shine.
Sing *Summertime* as one loud moan of pain
through the gravel and broken glass in your throat.
You know you got it if it makes you feel good.

Question Mark and the Mysterions

I'm upstairs in my teenage bedroom, lights out,
listening to WABC, Cousin Brucie,
under the covers, my hair so tightly wound
around wire rollers the size of juice cans
that it's impossible to sleep.
But how else can I get it to flow from the center
part, then flip at the ends in symmetrical s's?
How can I go to school, if my hair's not right?
Who will I fall in love with, who will take me
to the prom, *who wrote the book of love?*
I lean out the window, no streetlights
here in the country, just Orion's cinch belt,
Cassiopeia's W, the same letter I wear on my chest
when I cheer for the team, *All for you, Red*
and Blue. I'm the only one who can do a flip
and a cartwheel-split. *In the jungle, the mighty jungle,*
the lion sleeps tonight. . . . I wail along
in my tinny voice, unable to imagine a village
in Africa, children squatting in the dust,
but somehow I tap in to the small stream
of longing that floats off those high thin notes.
Out there in the night sky, the dusty river
of the Milky Way is flowing, pulsing
toward the future, where s's flip to question marks,
little fish hooks that bob and dip in the current,
go where it takes them.

Fortieth High School Reunion

The Friday night party's at an upscale bistro
on Main Street, but we remember
when it was The Busy Bee, where hatchet-faced
Agnes sold penny candy, wax lips, licorice whips,
fireballs that alternated hot and sweet as they grew
smaller, down to their fiery cores; an old dusty-
shelved dime store, where you could buy a stack
of comics, then walk home by yourself,
in the innocent fifties, when people burned
leaves at the curb, small smoldering fires,
air gritty with wood ash and leaf smoke . . . .

At the Saturday dinner dance, all of us dressed
in our best, black satin, spangles, sequins winking
with hidden fire, twisting to the tunes from the trio.
Smoke gets in your eyes.
Ten years from now, who knows where we'll be?

So let's raise a glass to Rich and Diana, who went
to the prom, then married other people, met again
on classsmates.com. Let's cheer for Charlie, class
clown, who dazzles on the dance floor with his
swing dance partner. Let's lift a cup of punch
to the kids in the creased photo of the kindergarten
circus: Sally, the tightrope walker, Mary Ann,
the clown, Richard, the ringmaster. Sara is gone,
and so is Carol, who died young, and Maggie,
tambourine in her lap and underpants showing,
who loved to ride motorcycles in the desert,
hot wind in her face, didn't see the darkness
ahead, that major stroke coming.

So we're out here dancing in the light, before
our arthritic knees lock up, and our eyes glaze
over with cataracts or glaucoma. The road is all
downhill now, for the class of sixty-three, the years
whizzing by like road signs, all arriving at the same
destination. What matters in the end is how well

we lived in that small space where the hyphen
goes. Remember the words scrawled in the margins
of our yearbook? *4 get me not.*
2 sweet 2 be 4 got 10. Good luck
to a good kid. Love, love, love.

Hard Bop

It's a sweet June day, and the mockingbirds
are singing, as are the rubber tires of cars
on the road, and both of these sounds reverberate,
echo, the jazz of early summer, with the muffled
percussion of wind in the trees. A crow
twangs and plucks his black guitar,
and I'm riffing along with the breeze, scatting
words here and there, trying to make sense
of my life, and the news of the world—
almost daily, another car bomb shatters
the desert, and hundreds of lives are torn
apart, as grief ripples outward in concentric
rings. Thomas Merton said, *God is that bit*
of diamond dust shining within each of us,
scraps of stardrift, our shared DNA. What
new language now needs to be born, a fusion
of birdsong and sandstorm, an improv
of heartbeat's ratatatat and moonbeam's
glissando? Crows in the road. Tires in the rain.

Rhythm Section

My son loves his rain stick, turns it over
and over, hearing the small beans
rolling down their grooves becoming
the rhythm of the summer rain
on the roof, all the windows open,
as we float off to sleep. He likes
other instruments as well,
has a doumbek whose skin
makes drum tones or heartbeats,
iambs for others to dance to.
At the piano, he plays the music
chimed by the chapel bells at college—
if we started running from the apartments
on Bishop Street, we could just make curfew
by the 11th bong. And there are the small bells
on a stick that he's shaking, music
from the neck of a goat, an alpine
meadow full of bluebells, buttercups,
daisies, or the clear gold notes
in church, when a circle of wheat
becomes the body of God, given
for all of us, even for him.

Gravy

To make good gravy, you must be patient,
let the juice settle to the bottom, let the fat
float to the top in all its golden light. Skim
it with a thin spoon, take its measure. Equal
it with flour, sprinkle with salt, speckle
with pepper. Stir constantly in the roasting pan,
making figure eights with a wooden spoon.
Scrape off strips of skin, bits of meat; incorporate
them in the mixture, like a difficult uncle
or the lonely neighbor invited out of duty.
Keep stirring. Hand the wooden baton
to one of your daughters; it's time for her
to start learning this music, the bubble
and seethe as it plays the score. One minute
at the boil, then almost like magic, it's *gravy,*
a rich velvet brown. Thin it with broth,
stir in chopped giblets, then pour into
its little boat, waiting with mouth open.
Take up your forks, slide potatoes, stuffing,
gravy, into your mouth, hum under your breath.
Oh, the holy family of gravy, all those
little odd bits and pieces, the parts that could
be discarded, but aren't; instead, transformed
into a warm brown blanket that makes
delicious every thing it covers.

Barbara Crooker is the author of one previous collection of poetry, *Radiance*, which won the 2005 Word Press First Book competition and was a finalist for the 2006 Paterson Poetry Prize. Her poems have appeared in many journals and anthologies, including *Good Poems For Hard Times; Sweeping Beauty: Contemporary Women Poets Do Housework; Red, White, and Blues in America;* and *Boomer Girls.* Her work has been featured on *Verse Daily* and read by Garrison Keillor on NPR's *The Writer's Almanac.* She is the recipient of three Pennsylvania Council on the Arts Creative Writing Fellowships, twenty-four Pushcart Prize nominations, and a number of other awards: the 2006 Ekphrastic Poetry Award from *Rosebud*, the 2004 WB Yeats Society of New York Award, the 2004 Pennsylvania Center for the Book Poetry in Public Places Poster Competition, the 2003 Thomas Merton Poetry of the Sacred Award, the 2003 "April Is the Cruelest Month" Award from Poets & Writers, the 2000 *New Millenium Writing's* Y2K competition, and the 1997 *Karamu* Poetry Award.

Printed in the United States
150633LV00004B/30/P

9 781933 456928